Girls Like Us

Girls Like Us

Elizabeth Hazen

Alan Squire Publishing
Bethesda, Maryland

Alan Squire Publishing

Girls Like Us is published by Alan Squire Publishing, Bethesda, MD, an imprint of the Santa Fe Writers Project.

Library of Congress Control Number: 2019956043

Printed in the United States of America.
ISBN (print): 978-1-942892-22-9
ISBN (epub): 978-1-942892-23-6

Jacket design by Randy Stanard, Dewitt Designs, www.dewittdesigns.com.
Cover collage by Lindsay Fleming.
Author photo by Amy Berbert.
Copy editing and interior design by Nita Congress.
Printing consultant: Steven Waxman.
Printed by API/Jostens.

First Edition
Ordo Vagorum

Acknowledgments

This book exists thanks to the guidance and support of numerous people. First, I owe a huge debt to Rose Solari and James Patterson of Alan Squire Publishing for their belief in my work and their incredible contributions to the creative lives of so many people. The entire ASP team have been patient and thoughtful collaborators; thank you Max Barton, Nita Congress, and Randy Stanard. Thanks to the Maryland State Arts Council for a grant that has allowed me time to finish a number of the poems included here. Thanks to my colleagues at Calvert School, who have encouraged me to pursue my work as a poet and allowed me to share my passion with our students; I am fortunate to spend my days with such talented people. And of course, thank you to my students for giving me purpose and perspective and for making me laugh.

Several friends read early versions of the poems here, as well as drafts of the entire manuscript, and that feedback was invaluable as I shaped and revised my vision of this book. Thanks to Jessica Blau, Betsy Boyd, Elisabeth Dahl, Jane Delury, Kathy Flann, Christine Grillo, Jim Magruder, Andrew Motion, and Marion Winik. You are generous readers, and I am grateful for your advice and your friendship.

I am extremely lucky to have parents who have been steadfast in their belief that I have something to say, and who have helped me find the time and voice to say it. Thank you, Robert and Margaret Hazen. Thank you to my brother, Ben Hazen, for your kindness and compassion. Thank you to my stepchildren, Atlas and Ramona, for allowing me to be in your lives. Thank you to my son, Greg, for your creativity, your passion, and the many ways you help me stay on track. And thank you to my husband, Grantley Pyke, for helping me shift the narrative.

***

I would like to acknowledge the following publications in which these poems first appeared:

American Literary Review: "The Bereaved"

Antigonish Review: "Death Valley"

Coachella Review: "Diagnosis I," "Diagnosis II," "Diagnosis III," "Scene from a Horror Movie"

The Common: "Devices," "Game Rules"

Dead Inside: "Why I Love Zombie Woman #6"

Ducts: "After He Calls Me a Low-Hanging Fruit," "Blackout"

Gargoyle: "Tips from a Nude Model," "Why I Love Zombie Woman #6"

The Hopkins Review: "Circling," "Imperatives"

One Hundred Word Stories: "The Clock"

Painted Bride Quarterly: "Eve at the Stop 'n' Shop"

Pair-Shaped: "Alignment," "Hide and Seek," "Lucky Girl," "Sea Plane"

The Potomac Review: "Photograph"

Sententia: "Against Resignation," "Diamond," "Free Fall," "Why I Love Laundry"

Shenandoah: "Monarch"

For all the girls we've been
and for Grantley

Contents

1

2

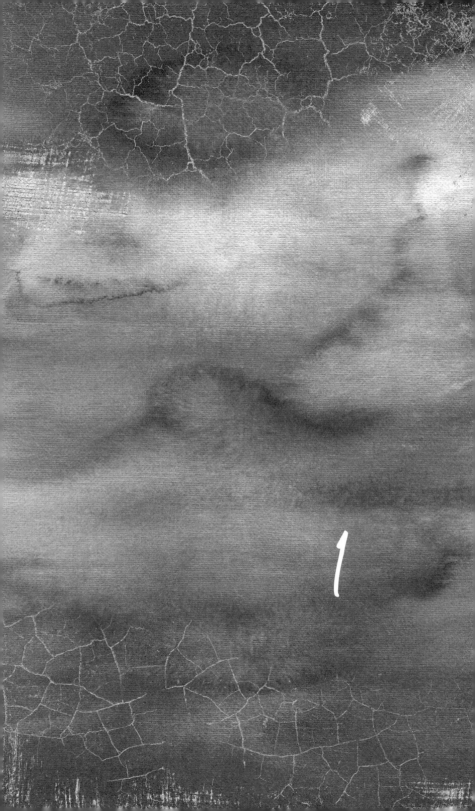

Devices

Rhyme relies on repetition: *pink drink,*
big wig, tramp stamp, rank skank. Alliteration

too: *Peter Piper's pickled peppers, silly*
Sally's sheep — *silly* trumping *smart* because

the *ll*s create consonance. Assonance
repeats vowel sounds: *hot bod, dumb slut, frigid bitch.*

Even his line — "Girl, we'll have a *fine time*" —
or her refusals — "*No! Don't!*" In metaphor

we compare two things. Suppose a man calls
a woman *fox*; we understand this is

not literal. Same goes for *pig, dog, chick.*
Same goes for *octopus*, as in, "His hands

were all over me." Metonymy relies
on association: *suits, skirts,* that joke

about the dishwasher — *If it stops working,*
slap the bitch! Synecdoche reduces

a thing to a single part: he wants *pussy,*
by which we must infer he wants a woman.

We've been called so many things that we are not,
we startle at the sound of our own names.

Against Resignation

after John Berryman

A blind brow above an empty heart is all
you thought you wanted. What simplicity
to be as silence or as air — there yet

not there. But it takes such work to disappear,
and secrets threaten to spill from you like liquor
you can't hold. You tell yourself you're someone else.

Though repeated lies become familiar
and safe, words are like labels, easily
removed; your clothes obstructions, easily

removed. Two wrongs don't make a right, but practice
perfects your expectations. Too many men
know where you live. Some nights you fear they'll come

for you; more nights you fear no one will come.
You are all sticks and bramble, a wicker girl,
a hazard. Women eye you up and down.

Men lick their lips. You could grow old in hiding,
resign to a shuttered room, but hope — cruel trick —
emboldens you, so you unlock your door.

Game Rules

In the rules you failed to learn from articles
in women's magazines; from your mother's loose-
lipped friends, those pseudo-aunts who snuck you schnapps

and cigarettes, reveled as you revealed
your indiscretions; or from too-fast girls
who disappeared midyear, birthing bastards

three states west of anywhere you'd been —
the gist was don't admit the things you need.
Back then you balked at such directives, though

in school you went along with rules, slicing right
into the porcine heart, the only girl
who didn't retch, so eager to see its rooms,

bloodless and gray, as if those spaces held
the recklessness that you could not contain.
Muscled walls, drained of mystery, labeled

in textbook diagrams — atrium, ventricle,
aortic valve — but you remember nothing
now, save the formaldehyde's choking fumes.

After the Argument

Your absence hovers,
a fox watching through
a thicket of chokeberry.
The stadium's roar rides
the breeze into our open
window; motors rage
up 83; an owl screams.

When did everything
devolve to noise?
The multitudes clamor,
cadence of their quarreling
predictable as pop songs.
When did this space
around me deepen

into trenches? I reapply
my lipstick, trace faces
in the dust that coats
the photograph of us when we
were young: you're poised
as if about to speak; I'm caught
in your silence.

Blackout

Blackout is the tear
in your dress. It is flashing

red and blue, the officer
guiding you to the curb.

Blackout is your car
crumpled, time lost between

the bar and this intersection.
Blackout is this crossroads.

Blackout is muscles
knowing what has happened,

but not how or when
or with whom.

Blackout is falling
into his bed, but before

his hands are on you,
you have faded away.

Blackout is lying, *Yes,*
I remember.

Blackout is absence:
a chipped tooth or prongs

of a setting that used to
grasp a gem.

Blackout is forgetting
where you left your shoes.

Blackout is for girls like us
who can be rearranged.

The Bereaved

I've grown so still, so scared and scarce as those
lost years when I was ill. The doctors say

I'm healthy now. I eat three squares and then some.
I haven't had a drink in months, in years,

in decades. Time, you know, is relative.
Even Saint Augustine lived in anxious

distraction, fingering beads of his rosary
just as I twist knots in my own hair. It was doubt

that first defined existence. Time itself
makes no assertion. Loss hits hardest, without

warning: notes in the margins of a book,
the careless loop of his *L*s. Defeated by

forgetting, I can't help but ask myself
if he was the one spared. That is the darkest

moment; then the thought is gone like exhaled
smoke, proof that I'm still breathing.

Tips from a Nude Model

If you sit still long enough, your ass can fall
asleep; the numbing will be gradual,

as curtains fade in light. Try not to worry
if you lose sensation; no one can hurry

the clock's progress. If your body wakes to pins,
you must ignore the pain — it's only skin

deep, after all — till he completes his sketch,
and *then* you may unfold yourself and stretch.

When you resume the pose, arms arced in place
above your head to create negative space,

select a focal point and fix your gaze.
It is useful to remember no one stays

statue-still. Don't forget to breathe. Don't let
him touch you. When the session ends, collect

your pay; insist on cash. Get dressed. Don't smile.
Know that your body may be numb awhile,

and when your see yourself revealed in paint,
note the proportions, but ignore the faint

glimmer he put in your eye that isn't you.
Embrace who you are, the nothing that you do.

Hide and Seek

In childhood, you believed everything
was waiting to be found.
Think of the rocks your father led you to,
the fossils inside; the basement

boxes spilling secrets: love
letters, photographs, cracked
china dolls, handkerchiefs stitched
with strange initials.

Think of the stillness
of your hiding place: your body
stretched so flat beneath the sheet,
a wrinkle alone betrayed you.

You dwindled. Protruding
bones became a shroud;
no one could see beyond
your hunger. Even now,

your low-cut dress, electric
blue and shining, reveals
nothing of consequence.
You spend whole seasons

hiding, emerging just to check
the mail, but your ear
is always cocked
for *Olly olly oxen free.*

Death Valley

My father grips the wheel.
My mother reads a map in darkness.

We are somewhere between

Flagstaff and Antelope Canyon.

I am somewhere between my brother
and the wheel well.

Jackrabbits play chase with our van, and I
am out of breath.

This morning, an invisible
rattle shook
but we carried on through oceans
of sagebrush and sand.

Back home, cicada shells cling to bark.
For weeks after our return I will pluck
the umber husks
and string them like trophies
to tie around my neck.

On the window I trace *Elizabeth* in the fog
of my breath.

By the time I reach the *h*, the *E*
has disappeared.

Diagnosis I

In Exam Room 3, I drank
barium sulfate through
a bendy straw, breast buds

rising beneath my hospital gown.
Sharp pangs like scissors
snipped inside me, but the x-ray

revealed no ulcers; in his preacher's
tenor, the doctor insisted
I had no cause for pain.

Diagnosis II

At the bus stop men sneered,
the "V" on my back like a wound
they claimed was theirs

to heal. The blades of their laughter
snipped my skin. They fed
me applejack, its heat

spreading, a numbing salve, until
their tongues' insistence
was akin to tenderness.

"V" on my back: A slang designation for girls believed to be virgins.

Diagnosis III

Girls like you, he spat,
his breath laden with smoke
and Svedka, his hands

rough stones. Thirty-seven
years old, and still a girl torn
and waiting, the old pain

blunt inside me. *Girls like
you*, he repeated, leaving me
a blank to fill.

Eve at the Stop 'n' Shop

There is a science
to my selection: I take two

of everything: artichokes
plastic bags of yellow corn

green beans   asparagus
a peach in each fist

My cart sinks:
nine gallons of milk

six dozen eggs
butter   sharp cheddar

burlap sacks of rice
boxes of pasta   jars of sauce

frozen peas crinkling
like static   I fill

three carts with TV dinners
two carts with cat food

a basket of steak vacuum-
sealed in cellophane

I carry a pack of
Doublemint gum

It takes four hours to ring
me up and six trips

to take everything home
The cabinets bulge

Goods ooze through cracks
Pots and pans ring

disbelief   I soothe them
with carrots   I add and add

The kitchen floods
with my mistakes   I have no one

to feed   I am starving
for broccoli florets

The room deep with dismay
thick with flour and meat

and all the recipes
I have failed to complete

The dishes rise to the ceiling
and fall   Soapy water

fills the room   I have
forgotten what it was

I wanted

After the Cocktail Party

The house is still
as winter. Waiting
in her bed, I watch reruns,

canned laughter crashing
through quiet, echoes
of departed guests.

Heartthrob Red on her
wineglass's rim; discarded
pantyhose; a smoothed-

out napkin, her scrawl
a cipher. Downstairs
I find her half-

dressed at the table,
face pressed in her bent
arm. The rooms sigh

with strange perfume;
my mother sleeps. Nothing
here is mine to keep.

After He Calls Me a Low-Hanging Fruit

I have a dream in
which I am staring
at the dead branches
of a black tree, bold
against blue sky.
On the highest branch
stands a girl in a red
school uniform.
I am mesmerized
by the intensity
of color, so I can't
be sure whether she
jumps or falls, but her
impact shakes me.
The red of her
uniform, red of her
blood — that heap
of red against
the grass looks,
to me, like apples.

Pastoral, September 1995

Everything rusted to a halt:
shutters split from hinges, gutters

plunge, roof like a hammock.
A two-dimensional boy on a swing

scarcely swaying, his face
as blank as a paper plate.

Quaint as a windmill, from the front
porch, a girl in coveralls

studies me. The smoke from my
Camel twirls from the window,

just as I practiced all summer.
I drive past a row of muscle cars

spilling parts, field after field cut
to stalk, and not a cloud in sight.

Drown

Mistaking immediacy for
intimacy, I frame my thoughts
of men in future tense,

trying romantic turns
of text as one tests the warmth
of breaking surf. I insist

on shifting the narrative: no
more numbing loneliness
with 80-proof answers to *What*

do I do now? No more being
that kind of girl — yet I wake
up in strange beds as from

dreams in which huge waves
are hands that press down on
my neck, assuring me *You can*

breathe down here. But I
can't breathe under water,
and neither can I drown.

Dictation

After days of heavy drinking, blackout

is swift and total. Mexico, the moon so huge
and blank, a hole of perfect darkness

punched out. You wake up aching. Sand plasters your left ear.

> *How like a doll you were, how yielding.*
> *I could have done anything I wanted.*

With a ragged fingernail, you scrape
the sand that cakes your ear.

Your thirst dictates silence. *Anything I wanted.*

> *But I decided not to.*
Decisive. Incisive. *He* decided.

And are you not the one who wanted him

to stiffen up the drinks? Are you not the one
who fell? But *he* decided.

You practice arguments on your own body.

A different voice repeating:

Unclamp your tongue.

The Clock

The month she asks him to leave there are signs: earthquake, hurricane, a dead rabbit on the threshold. In retellings, she will claim to have buried the corpse, but in truth she scoops it with a shovel, puts it out with the next day's trash. For weeks she arranges and rearranges piles — plates, cutlery, bedding, photographs — as if solving a complex equation. The day of his departure, the mantel clock stops. Inside, the dead cell oozes into gears, and though she scrapes away the corrosion, a new battery is not enough, and the hours pass, though not exactly as before.

Letter from My Father (after his brother's death)

A rockfish head, a gull,
a bug-eyed carp twitching

in the surf, stench of
putrefaction everywhere.

Coiled at the base of
the cliff's highest point,

a copperhead tensed
and hissing: high tide

imminent, nothing
to be done. Still worse,

a whale skull emerging
from the rock face

destroyed by plundering
amateurs. This loss

cannot be quantified.
Near the car, a groundhog,

mortally wounded by
osprey talon, growls.

I give her a wide berth.
What else could be done?

Diamond

Engendering myths of shattered stars the diamond,
too, is born of pressure. The derivation
of the word is Greek *adamao* — "I tame,"
but the ring he gave me failed to keep me

pacified. Our forms are carbon-based, but if
emotions have no substance, how can anger
tense the features of my face? How do words —
lacking form beyond the curve of font, the flick

of tongue, the measure of my breathing — break,
so easily, a bond? I fear my heart
has grown impenetrable; I skim his letters
but make no reply. Synthetic diamonds ground

to dust are used in blades that cut through steel;
this I understand. Too well, in fact, I've learned
how easily we manufacture might,
how quick we redirect our strength to sever.

Moving Day

We knocked a hole in the wall
with the sofa foot, and I bruised

my thigh and sprained my thumb.

Between my old house and his,
the truckload shifted and broke

my lamp. No matter; my excess crowds

the garage: chairs, paintings, mismatched
plates, my superfluous coffee maker.

I too am a redundancy; his children

close their doors. My mind's
an emptied drawer, its clutter filed away.

My wedding dress, sheathed

in plastic, hangs beside costumes
from long-ago parties. Boxes surround me

like fortifications — we consolidate

our spices, cull duplicates from our bookshelves.
I keep the copies that were mine,

my marginal scrawls like relics.

Monster

Just now a sudden
                    ruckus thrusts me from dreaming

into darkness
                    like the snow
                                        of an old TV set,

        a hangover's persistent whine.

Stacks of scrapbooks
                        tower like cairns.

            The rattle at my window
beckons like a dare:
                    an opossum,

                    glass between us cellophane
                                        then mirror.

I cry out. I close
                    the curtain,
pull it back.

In the carport floodlight,
                        teeth like dripping needles.

                        Remnants of my last few meals
                                    litter the concrete.

I bang the glass

        with my palms, then flatten

        myself into bed.

If I can't see her

                I tell myself

        she isn't there.

Lucky Girl

Everyone reassures me that I'm not
as bad as the worst thing
I've done. Nothing

is ever black and white.
Even the made bed is just
a precursor to disorder.

I must remember *good*
is just a word. *Beauty, success,*
happiness. It's hard to resist

the seduction of a lie,
the way it tastes like whiskey, dark
and heavy, the tongue

of a working man after
his shift. I wake up groggy;
I nod and smile. A man says something

about *a girl like you* and *a place*
like this, but I can't see
where I am, or who.

Taps, August 1984

At dusk my mother pulled the eyelet
curtains closed and smoothed me into bed.

Behind our house the Naval Hospital lurked,
an uninvited guest. The recorded bugle's lone

notes marked the passing of another day;
darkness spread. My father with his trumpet

played along. Night never failed to enter,
rearranging shadows. Our grandfather

clock struck the quarter hour; the blades of
the ceiling fan cut summer's thickness;

my mother clinked her ice. Mercy was
the smallness of my world. Soldiers paced

the perimeter. My bed was a dingy, my shag rug
a wild sea. The dirge became an anthem,

and I a warrior, uncertain of her foe.
Three decades on, two vodka sodas into

my afternoon, I watch a military funeral
on the TV above the bar. The bartender

buys me another round. I drink away
daylight, chat about war and weather.

Addict

Every time I bite my tongue,
I seem to grow another one,

glossing over past mistakes,
vows I didn't mean to break.

In neon glow of game show sets,
contestants place their sucker bets;

like them I rally, spin the wheel,
instruct myself on what to feel.

I've learned a thousand ways to lie,
but patience seems to pass me by.

I am conflicted; thick with gin.
I can't remember where I've been.

Resentful of the task of choosing,
I find in choice I'm always losing.

My expectations are my curse;
desire only makes things worse.

Conspirator, even in sleep,
each word a promise I won't keep.

Free Fall

In cartoons gravity waits for recognition —
the long pause while Wile E. lingers mid-

air before grasping his predicament.
He scrambles just beyond the precipice,

then plummets through branches or shelves of stone
to crash in a heap, but only briefly broken.

Last night the edge was looming like horizon,
and I felt myself compelled as though carried by tide.

The moon's pull is nothing compared to the weight
of my body sinking into his bed again.

The acceleration of a falling object
occurs at a constant rate, and repetition

changes nothing unless conditions change.
I crave the moment when no choice is left

to make, when no reaction can alter fate,
and, for a moment, I can disappear.

Why I Love Laundry

In the days just after breaking up, the laundry
tallies the time that's passed since you had him
in your bed, reminds you this despair is young,
proves you can, in fact, wash some things away.
From the metallic drum you pull the panties
he slid a final time, from hips to ankles.

The number of remaining pairs accounts
for days that followed, days you ached for him,
revising history. A week from now,
you will be ready to move on from this,
and like the t-shirts, gone through the wringer
a hundred times, his face will start to fade.

In this mechanical dirge you find solace,
knowing that for every man you ever left
or who left you, there is this repetition
you can count on: the ritual of cleansing
sheets of their scents, their DNA; the grace
of this machine, so modest in design.

Alignment

Planets align from time to time, and much
is made of the effects such cosmic chance
could have on Earth, though in fact the influence
is trivial; such coincidence can't touch

the craft of carpenters with their dovetail
joints, welders with their pipes, mechanics
with their wheels and calibrations. There's no trick
to their creations; precision must avail.

And what of the body? The chiropractor
tries to understand my pain, tries to adjust
my vertebrae, but the problem is my lust's
incongruity with logic, a factor

that has no easy fix. I try to assuage
my desires by design, but now I find
myself off-kilter, haphazard, misaligned —
I fear I've gone too far to disengage.

These emotions don't fit naturally in place.
I want to rearrange my heart, to alter
the facts, selectively recall — I falter,
fall out of line, think only of his face.

Laceyville, PA

Plaster children in scraggy yards,
fields of ocher metal,

a mattress pressed in a window,
a sinking family plot.

You husk corn. I smoke,
clouding distant cattle.

We eat facing west.
A colony of bats screeches

toward water. One swoops
so close, I upset the wine;

rivulets spill through
slats of the table, staining

the sun-bleached deck.
We find another bottle, wait

for dark to fall and
settle things.

Photograph

The question of the photograph concerns
your easy heart, the reckless optimism

that leads you to believe, with each new love,
This time will be different. The question

of the photograph is math that won't add up.
You recognize the lake, your son's hand in yours

as you leap together off the dock, bodies
braced for cold, captured midair by an invisible

finger's clicking. You remember your son's
sticky grip, his squeals, the way he reached for you

underwater. You remember the splash,
the shivering aftermath, but nothing of

the one who caught you there. He left no trace
but an edge of shadow, the picture's only flaw.

Sea Plane

In childhood games
of hide and seek we left
our shoes as decoys
at the foot of floor-length drapes.
How hastily we fill in any blanks.

Think of that baby picture,
your extended hand;
the flash obscured my face,
but still our mother marvels
at those smiles.

In a photograph taken
decades before our births,
a sea plane tilts forty-five degrees,
though in ascent or falling,
we've never been sure.

Circling

Through lattice under
the porch of a condemned

house, a feral cat sizes
me up. A barstool's metal foot

scrapes the tacky floor,
expletive cracking the din.

Every street corner blinks
delicious permission:

neon invitations, pillow-
talk promises, smiling

strangers in drugstore
picture frames. I circle

the block, waiting for a sign:
rock star parking outside

Club Charles or a green light
to usher me home?

Each day thirst churns
inside me, my fulcrum

teetering. Each day victory
feels more like delay.

Scene from a Horror Movie

Her breasts heave, thrusting
cleavage into slants

of glowing blue, and through
her cotton nightgown

you see her nipples wink.
I watch the wash

of eerie light accentuate
the dark between her

girlish thighs. Someone
with leather gloves

reflected in a knife.
Her legs are long and slender;

each frame shortens
her nightie. Tension mounts;

the killer strikes, and she grasps
at nothing, her face

warping like a rubber mask;
her body shudders.

A gasp like hard candy
catches in my throat.

Love Poem

I love you changes me
into a tree falling

after erosion has its say.
This process does not

simply take away
the cliff's edge — it creates

new space, frees me
from fear of stasis.

It tells me I'm still
young enough to be

surprised. I first believed
the tree was dead,

but months later
it blossomed, this emblem

of possibility prostrate
across our path,

this tangle of limbs
like a castaway

clawing her way back
from the sea.

Why I Love Zombie Woman #6

Because she's stuck with rigor-mortised legs
and decomposing skin, but perseveres;
because she sees without eyeballs, she hears
with oozing ears; because her organs, like eggs
dropped from their carton, hit the path with *splats*,
but still she trudges on; because her need
is clear, uncomplicated: she must feed;
because she barely notices the rats
that gnaw her ankles; because she doesn't stop,
even after the hatchet hacks clean through
her reaching arm; because she will pursue
her prey till they have nothing left to chop.
Because when she lies in pieces, inside out,
she will not know regret, or shame, or doubt.

Driving Home at Dawn

Sunday's sunrise traffic
lights are quaint

formalities, the sky
a blushing promise

the universe will keep.
Before I left, you

clutched my mess of hair.
I took your scent —

maple syrup, sweat, smoke.
All morning my own

skin rioted with it. Even now,
my fingertips tingle,

your name like a host
on my tongue.

The Himitsu-Bako
(Personal Secret Box)

Unless you know the secret steps, the box

remains impenetrable. There is no latch,

no key, no lid, or flaps to fold. Untrained

eyes see no inside; it is a tchotchke,

a conversation piece, as purposeless

as a cracked glass. But a closer look reveals

a maze of moving parts, intricate machineries;

in deft hands the box blooms — origami rose

or child's fortune teller. Its emptiness

becomes its promise, vast as a blank page.

Dream

A hummingbird trapped
inside a feeder

beats her wings against
the glass. I think

maybe I can free
her, so I carry the feeder

through a maze of locked
doors. I unscrew the lid.

An anticlimax of
release, she flaps just

as before, but stays
improbably in place.

A voice repeats:
Just open your eyes.

Electricity

of my mother's
touch woke the surface of

my skin, generating
heat, deepening my color.

She charged the inside
of my arm, marble smooth

and tingling from wrist
to elbow crook. I froze as if

movement might frighten
her away, but still,

there was no keeping her.
Now, my own strumming

fingers soothe my son,
though my mind's a clutter

of charges, eighty wingbeats
per second. I lie until his

breath deepens and the ticking
clock becomes a heartbeat.

Imperatives

1.

Once we found a Great White tooth
as long as my son's thumb.
Once we dragged a jellyfish
to shore and watched it throbbing
like a huge, transparent heart.
Once we stayed in pajamas
for five days, waiting out the snow.
Last week, a brown-headed cowbird,
dead beside our door.
Three days later I dumped
the corpse behind the shed.

2.

Chlorine smell catches in
his shaggy hair. Yesterday's stale
coffee, the slant of rain
that wets my windowsill, the shoes
he outgrew months ago, but
I refuse to throw away.

3.

Braced teeth and tangle
of preteen limbs vamp
for the camera, caught

squinting or midlaugh or barely
there, just a halo of red hair hovering
in the back or a crown of
green goggles bobbing: my son,
unsmiling; the family curse
might skip him, this inward-
turning darkness.

4.

My father took me early
to feed the science teacher's
brown anoles who ate live mealworms,
wriggling golden larvae
packed in wheat bran,
the smell of which still makes me gag.
Once I found a lizard
corpse, part cannibalized, part
decayed. Two days later,
wisps of skeleton, filigree of bone.

5.

Brown-headed cowbirds lay
eggs in others' nests, abandoning
their young. Brown anoles eat
their molted skin. Sometimes
they eat their tails. Sometimes
they eat their young. My skin
is as thin as testa — seed coat
beneath a cracked shell.

Just Things

Is the act of fixing a smashed-in back door
no more than a repair? The broken glass
no more than the result of thoughtless thieves?

You shim the threshold while I survey the yard:
Virginia creepers rise like plumes of smoke
to suffocate the pines. One graceless yank

is all it takes to upset a nest — a nest
so neatly woven, so perfectly nest-like,
it seems to me a prop. And being June,

the nest spills eggs as smooth and blue as plastic.
I put things back the way they were, save
the cracked egg smeared on the weed-choked lawn.

What if the door means nothing beyond passage?
The deadbolt protects my frame of mind alone,
and the nest's proximity to my house is

just coincidence? I ask you if my child
will be safe now, the house secure. You hold
your tongue. This universe is riddled with fists,

false logic, eggshells, viscera, regret.
Am I forgiven? Will you answer that?
Can anyone tell me what I'm meant to do?

Monarch

A monarch butterfly fallen from the air
lay in a field. I took her home, pinned her

to the wall above my desk. For five years
she was part of the scenery, like the tea-

cup my son painted, or like the Post-it note
you left once, slipping out before I woke:

I love you scrawled in Sharpie. I took for granted
her orange-rind, stained-glass wings, slanted

bolts of black the texture of velvet
paintings, white spots along the edge like eyelets.

I moved in with you gradually, a few boxes
each weekend for months. I moved the monarch

toward the end, in a frenzy of packing and lifting.
I was careless with her, tossed her without thinking

into a liquor box filled with books, the spines
uneven hazards. That she was mine

to protect had not occurred to me before
I opened the box to find the right wing torn,

so all that was left was her body,
the other wing, and orange flecks like confetti

that I shook out over my empty desk, brushed
into my palm, and let fall into the trash.

I was certain she was beyond repair,
but now that she's gone, I see her everywhere.